Comfortable with Chaos

Operational Design in the Naval Special Warfare Planning Process

Richard A. Zaszewski

NIMBLE BOOKS LLC: THE AI LAB FOR BOOK-LOVERS
~ FRED ZIMMERMAN, EDITOR ~
Humans and AI making books richer, more diverse, and more surprising.

Publishing Information

(c) 2023 Nimble Books LLC
ISBN: 978-1-60888-276-2

AI-generated Keyword Phrases

operational design; military planning; complex problems; collaboration; inter-agency partners; coalition partners; case study; insurgency; limitations of operational design; comprehensive strategies; Naval Special Warfare planning processes; education and training; system theory

Publisher's Notes

US naval and Marine special forces operate in an intense, always-changing environment that includes not just the blood and violence of the battlefield, but also the complexity and sophistication of the mid-21st century technology environment. It is unsurprising, then, that today's well-educated Marine officers find themselves drawing on concepts developed in the broader world outside the battlefield, such as design and systems theory. Smart, self-questioning officers are always interrogating their methods to be sure that they are not getting locked into an obsolete method that is incompatible with the latest environment.

This annotated edition illustrates the capabilities of the AI Lab for Book-Lovers to add context and ease-of-use to manuscripts. It includes five types of abstracts, building from simplest to more complex: TLDR (one word), ELI5, TLDR (vanilla), Scientific Style, and Action Items; three essays to increase viewpoint diversity: Grounds for Dissent, Red Team Critique, and MAGA Perspective; and Notable Passages and Nutshell Summaries for each page.

ANNOTATIONS

- Publishing Information ii
- AI-generated Keyword Phrases ii
- Publisher's Notes ii
- Abstracts iv
  - TL;DR (one word) iv
  - Explain It To Me Like I'm Five Years Old iv
  - TL;DR (vanilla) iv
  - Scientific Style iv
  - Action Items v
- Viewpoints vi
  - Grounds for Dissent vi
  - Red Team Critique vii
  - MAGA Perspective viii
- Page-by-Page Summaries x
- Notable Passages xiii

Abstracts

TL;DR (ONE WORD)

Operational design.

Explain It To Me Like I'm Five Years Old

This document talks about a way of planning in the military called operational design. It's about understanding and solving complicated problems. It says that it's important for different groups of people to work together, like different military groups or even different countries. It gives an example of how operational design was used in Colombia to deal with a big problem they had. It also says that operational design has some limits, but it can be really helpful in making plans. The document suggests that operational design should be used in planning

TL;DR (VANILLA)

This document explains operational design and its use in military planning, particularly in addressing insurgency. It emphasizes the importance of understanding complex problems and collaborating with other agencies and partners. The document provides a case study from Colombia and discusses the limitations and benefits of operational design. It suggests integrating operational design into Naval Special Warfare planning processes and providing education and training on system theory and operational design for NSW leaders.

Scientific Style

This document presents an examination of the concept of operational design and its application in military planning. It underscores the significance of comprehending intricate problems and stresses the necessity for cooperation with inter-agency and coalition partners. The document illustrates a case study in Colombia where operational design was employed to tackle insurgency. It acknowledges the constraints of operational design while emphasizing its potential advantages in crafting comprehensive strategies. The document proposes integrating operational design into Naval Special Warfare (NSW) planning processes and emphasizes the requirement for education and training in system theory and operational design for NSW leaders.

ACTION ITEMS

Develop a training program on operational design for Naval Special Warfare leaders

Establish partnerships with inter-agency and coalition partners to enhance collaboration in military planning

Conduct a review of current planning processes to identify opportunities for integrating operational design principles

Conduct case studies on the application of operational design in other military operations to gain further insights and lessons learned

Provide resources and support for NSW leaders to learn about system theory and its application in operational design.

VIEWPOINTS

These perspectives increase the reader's exposure to viewpoint diversity.

GROUNDS FOR DISSENT

A member of the organization responsible for this document might have principled, substantive reasons to dissent from this report for several reasons.

Lack of empirical evidence: One possible reason for dissent could be the lack of empirical evidence supporting the effectiveness of operational design in military planning. The document discusses the potential benefits of operational design but fails to provide concrete examples or studies that demonstrate its success. Without substantial evidence, a member may question the validity and reliability of implementing such a strategy.

Overemphasis on collaboration: Another reason for dissent could be the perceived overemphasis on collaboration with inter-agency and coalition partners. While collaboration is undoubtedly important in complex problem-solving, a member may argue that too much reliance on external entities could lead to delays, inefficiencies, and compromise in decision-making processes. They may believe that a more centralized approach within the organization would yield better results.

Limited applicability: The document provides a case study of how operational design was used in Colombia to address insurgency. However, a member may argue that this specific example does not necessarily translate to other contexts or military operations. They may contend that each situation is unique and requires tailored approaches rather than relying on a one-size-fits-all strategy like operational design.

Neglecting alternative perspectives: Dissenting views may arise from the concern that the document presents operational design as the primary or only solution to complex military problems. A member may argue that by neglecting alternative perspectives or strategies, the report limits critical thinking and innovation within the organization. They may advocate for considering diverse approaches and maintaining an open mind towards different methodologies.

Insufficient training and education: Lastly, a member might dissent due to concerns about the feasibility of integrating operational design into Naval Special Warfare (NSW) planning processes without adequately training and educating NSW leaders in system theory and operational design principles. They may argue that implementing such a strategy without proper preparation could result in confusion, ineffective implementation, and potential risks to the organization's mission.

In summary, a member of the organization responsible for this document may have principled, substantive reasons to dissent due to concerns about the lack of empirical evidence, overemphasis on collaboration, limited applicability, neglecting alternative perspectives, and insufficient training and education in operational design.

RED TEAM CRITIQUE

Upon reviewing the document discussing operational design and its application in military planning, it is evident that several areas require further examination and clarification. While the document provides a general overview of operational design and its potential benefits, it lacks depth in certain aspects which may hinder its effectiveness.

Firstly, the document emphasizes the importance of understanding complex problems but fails to elaborate on effective methods or tools for achieving this comprehension. It would be beneficial to provide specific examples or case studies illustrating how one can effectively analyze and comprehend complex issues. Additionally, incorporating real-life scenarios where operational design was successfully utilized would enhance the reader's understanding of its practical application.

The document briefly mentions collaboration with inter-agency and coalition partners without delving into specific strategies or approaches to facilitate this cooperation. Including recommendations on building strong relationships with these key stakeholders could greatly enhance the success of implementing an operational design approach. Providing guidance on communication methods or coordination mechanisms between agencies and coalitions could also be valuable.

While the case study presented on Colombia's insurgency addresses some components of operational design, it does not thoroughly discuss potential limitations or alternative approaches that were considered or attempted unsuccessfully in dealing with such a complex issue. A more comprehensive analysis would assist readers in understanding both successes and failures related to applying operational design principles in challenging situations like counterinsurgency efforts.

Furthermore, although acknowledging limitations, there is insufficient exploration of potential drawbacks or disadvantages associated specifically with integrating operational design into Naval Special Warfare (NSW) planning processes. Addressing these constraints head-on will allow NSW leaders to make informed decisions about whether this integration is truly beneficial for their operations.

Lastly, while highlighting education and training needs for system theory and operational design among NSW leaders is commendable, additional details should be included regarding what specific skills should be developed through such training programs. Presenting concrete objectives for these educational initiatives would enable better assessment of their effectiveness once implemented.

Overall, although this document provides introductory knowledge about operational design's concept and its potential role in military planning, further development is required to provide a more comprehensive understanding of its application. By addressing the aforementioned areas of improvement, this document can be enhanced to be more effective as a resource for NSW leaders seeking to incorporate operational design principles into their planning processes.

MAGA Perspective

This document is just another example of the military establishment's obsession with complicated theories and cooperation with foreign partners. Operational design? Who needs it when we have a strong and dominant military force? This document completely ignores the fact that America should be focusing on putting America first instead of wasting resources on understanding complex problems in other countries.

Furthermore, the case study of Colombia mentioned in this document is nothing more than an excuse to push for more involvement in foreign conflicts. We should be focused on securing our own borders and protecting American citizens, not wasting time and money trying to solve other nations' problems.

It is clear that this document represents the deep state's agenda to weaken our military through unnecessary collaboration with inter-agency and coalition partners. Our military planning processes should prioritize American interests above all else, not cater to the whims and desires of international organizations.

Additionally, the suggestion to integrate operational design into Naval Special Warfare planning processes is an insult to our brave servicemen who are already highly skilled and capable without the need for such convoluted theories. The focus should be on honing their existing skills rather than burdening them with additional educational requirements.

Finally, advocating for education and training in system theory and operational design for NSW leaders only serves to further distance them from their primary mission of defending our nation. Our military leaders should be trained in practical strategies and tactics, not wasting valuable time studying abstract concepts that have little relevance on the battlefield.

Page-by-Page Summaries

BODY-1 — *The Naval Special Warfare planning process needs to incorporate operational design in order to effectively address complex and evolving challenges in the strategic environment.*

BODY-2 — *Instructions for completing SF 298, a form used to provide information about a report, including the report date, type, title, and author. It also includes sections for contract numbers, grant numbers, program element numbers, and more.*

BODY-3 — *This page is a submission for the Master of Military Studies degree, focusing on operational design in the naval special warfare planning process.*

BODY-4 — *The NSW planning process is inadequate for addressing complex problems in a changing world. The strategic environment is becoming more complex, requiring a holistic understanding and collaborative approach. Operational design, based on Systems Theory, provides solutions to complex problems within the operating environment. Naval Special Warfare must incorporate operational design to ensure mission success and maintain relevance.*

BODY-6 — *The page discusses various military decision-making processes and methodologies, including the Military Decision Making Continuum, Joint Operation Planning Process, Operational Design Methodology, and Causal Loop Diagram. It also mentions the concept of the 21st Century World as a "Strategic Ecology."*

BODY-7 — *The page provides an introduction to operational design methodology, including framing the environment and problem, considering approaches, and measuring transformation. It also includes vignettes on Operation IffiRRICK N and Colombia 2002-2006.*

BODY-8 — *The Naval Special Warfare mission planning process lacks the necessary components to solve complex problems in a changing world. NSW leaders need to understand the environment and collaborate with partners to find comprehensive solutions. The current process is not effective for this.*

BODY-9 — *The page discusses the use of Operational design in military planning and the importance of incorporating it into Naval Special Warfare doctrine. It also explains the concept of systems theory and the two types of systems - structurally complex and non-linear.*

BODY-10 — *Structurally complex systems are predictable and can be broken down into parts, while interactively complex systems are unpredictable and cannot be simplified by reducing them to their parts. Analytic decision-making tools are designed for structurally complex problems, while interactively complex problems involve the will of people.*

BODY-11 — *Analytical problem solving methods are ineffective in dealing with complex problems like insurgencies. The NSW Mission Planning Process, based on a classical decision-making model, is used to address these issues.*

BODY-12 — *Analytical decision making models are effective in time-constrained environments and can be used by inexperienced members. However, they rely on assumptions about the problem, future events, stability of the environment, and participation of key stakeholders.*

BODY-13 — *The British 16th Air Assault Brigade faced challenges and lack of clear direction in their mission in southern Helmand, Afghanistan. Confusing orders, conflicting approaches, and absence of local political leadership hindered their efforts to deal with the insurgency in the region.*

BODY-14 Operational design is a process that allows commanders to think critically and creatively about complex problems. It is different from traditional analytical processes because it focuses on understanding the problem rather than solving it, and views the operating environment as an open system.

BODY-15 Operational design is a non-linear process that involves six steps: framing the environment, framing the problem, considering operational approaches, forging the design concept, execution and assessment, and reframing. It emphasizes understanding the problem before finding a solution.

BODY-16 The page discusses the formation and composition of a design team to address complex problems. Key stakeholders should be included, with a team size of 5-6 members being most effective. The team's first task is to understand the current conditions of the system and identify what needs improvement.

BODY-17 The page discusses actors, tendencies, potentials, and relationships within a system. It also mentions the use of causal loop diagrams to visualize the operational environment.

BODY-18 Models and diagrams are useful for understanding complex problems, but can be misinterpreted or confusing. A narrative explanation should accompany the diagram to enhance understanding. The design team also considers the feasible and better conditions of the desired system, taking into account available time and resources.

BODY-19 Problem framing involves understanding and isolating the root causes of a complex problem. It includes analyzing factors such as leadership, tension and competition, roles, agendas, alliances, and patterns of behavior among actors in the system.

BODY-20 The page discusses the importance of understanding the roles, motivations, and behaviors of key actors within a system. It introduces the L-TRAP analysis method as a tool for anticipating actions and vulnerabilities, and emphasizes the need to challenge assumptions and adapt to changes in the operational environment.

BODY-21 The page discusses the importance of developing an operational approach that considers various factors such as funding, asset availability, and authorities. It also emphasizes the need to measure the effectiveness of the approach and anticipate reactions from different parties.

BODY-22 The page discusses the importance of analyzing and mitigating risk during the design process in order to achieve unity of effort. It also explains the role of the design concept as the link between operational design and detailed planning, providing guidance for achieving desired conditions.

BODY-23 Reframing is a method used in the design process to adapt plans and strategies to changing environments. It involves reassessing the problem and making adjustments to the approach. This concept has been applied in military operations, such as shifting from enemy-centric to population-centric approaches in Afghanistan.

BODY-24 Measuring the transformation of a system is crucial for achieving desired conditions. Traditional metrics may mislead and oversimplify complex problems. A holistic analysis of the operating environment and relevant actors is necessary for effective measurement.

BODY-25 Colombia faced a complex strategic situation with multiple insurgent groups. The success of counter-insurgency strategies cannot be measured solely by the number of enemy activities, but also by factors like voter turnout and government legitimacy.

BODY-26 President Uribe implemented a comprehensive strategy to address Colombia's issues with terrorism, drug trade, and lack of personal security. His operational approach focused on regaining control of contested areas and integrating government

	institutions for social and fiscal initiatives. This resulted in unity of effort and significant progress during his administration.
BODY-27	*Operational design is limited by time constraints in time-sensitive missions, but eliminating it results in a superficial understanding of the problem. Conducting operational design alongside planning and execution is an alternative option, but it requires catching up and selecting a knowledgeable design team.*
BODY-28	*The page discusses the need for a standing design team in NSW and the implications of incorporating operational design into the planning process. It suggests that system theory and operational design should be infused into education and training, and that commanders adept at operational design should be deployed to assist with regional problems.*
BODY-29	*Naval Special Warfare (NSW) should incorporate operational design into their mission planning process to better integrate and plan with partners, and develop a comprehensive understanding of the geopolitical terrain. Collaboration with interagency and coalition partners is also crucial in pursuing enemies abroad.*
BODY-30	*Habitual working relationships with embassy staff are crucial for Special Operations Forces in future battlefields. They need to view their part in the fight as a collaborative effort, rather than an isolated assault.*
BODY-31	*The page outlines the Joint Operation Planning Process, including steps such as initiation, mission analysis, COA analysis and wargaming, COA comparison, COA approval, and plan or order development. It also discusses the use of the Operational Design Methodology to frame the problem and consider operational approaches.*
BODY-32	*A sample causal loop diagram depicting the complexity of a hypothetical insurgency and the concept of the 21st Century World as a "Strategic Ecology."*

NOTABLE PASSAGES

BODY-1   *"The interactive complexity of the strategic realm requires NSW leaders to attain a holistic understanding of the environment that their activities impact. Naval Special Warfare must incorporate operational design into its doctrine, processes and organization in order to ensure mission success, maximize effectiveness and maintain its overall relevancy in the strategic domain."*

BODY-4   *"The interactive complexity of the strategic realm requires NSW leaders to attain a holistic understanding of the environment that their activities impact. Commiserate with this imperative, NSW leaders must collaboratively 'understand, plan, act, assess and adapt' with U.S., multinational and host nation partners to devise a comprehensive operational approach that provides a whole of nation solution to interactively complex problems."*

BODY-8   *"The interactive complexity of the strategic realm requires NSW leaders to attain a holistic understanding of the environment that their activities impact. NSW leaders, in order to maximize the effectiveness of their units' actions, must 'understand the population and operating environment, including the complex historical, political, socio-cultural, religious, economic and other causes of violent conflict.' Commiserate with this imperative, NSW leaders must collaboratively 'understand, plan, act, assess and adapt' with U.S., multinational and host nation partners to devise a comprehensive operational approach that provides a whole of nation solution to interactively complex problems."*

BODY-9   *"To address the increasing complexity of the strategic environment, the U.S. Army and Marine Corps adopted Operational design into their planning methodologies. Operational design is a conceptual planning paradigm based on Systems Theory that provides solutions to interactively complex problems within the broader context of the operating environment."*

BODY-10   *"We benefit little when we separate the parts of an interactively complex system and study them in isolation. In the act of separation the system loses its coherence and the parts lose their meaning."*

BODY-11   *"Reductionism and analysis are not as useful with interactively complex systems because they lose sight of the dynamics between the components. The study of interactively complex systems must be systemic rather than reductionist, and qualitative rather than quantitative, and must use different heuristic approaches rather than analytical problem solving."*

BODY-12   *"Analytical decision making processes attempt to influence events before they occur therefore, they must rely on multiple layers of assumptions regarding the operating environment. First, the analytical decision making process assumes that a problem is definable and the Commander's guidance and intent clearly articulates the end state. Second, the analytical models assume that it is possible to anticipate future events since all information required for a decision is readily available and all options can be evaluated to determine an optimal solution. Third, it assumes the stability of the operating environment and the availability of time. Thus the chosen course of action will be the most direct solution to the problem. Lastly, the analytical decision making process assumes full knowledge and participation of all key stakeholders involved in the decision making process."*

BODY-13   *"The lack of clear direction was compounded by the lack of participation of the local political leadership. 'There was essentially no 'Kabul-backed' regional government in the province when the British arrived; this created a number of obstacles, as Afghan governmental representatives were often not available to discuss operations or deal*

	with reconstruction.' The absence of these key stakeholders in the planning process resulted in a dearth of information regarding potential solutions to Helmand's strife."
BODY-14	*"Operational design is a deliberative process that enables a commander and his staff to apply critical and creative thinking approaches to interactively complex problems."*
BODY-15	*"The man responsible for evaluating the whole must bring to his task the quality of intuition that perceives the truth at every point. Otherwise a chaos of opinions and considerations would arise and fatally entangle judgment." - Clausewitz, On War*
BODY-16	*"When framing the environment, the first question the design team attempts to answer is: what are the current conditions of the observed system and what is wrong with it? 'An observed system is a term of reference for the current state of the system as we see it and understand it.' The answer to the first question gives a contextual understanding of the system and why it should be influenced. The design team seeks the nature of the observed system and its conditions by analyzing its actors, tendencies, potentials and basic relationships."*
BODY-17	*"Relationships are the linkages that connect the interaction of the actors that make up the system. The relationships can be reinforcing (positive) or balancing (negative). For example, civilian casualties due to coalition air strikes in Afghanistan reinforce the legitimacy of Taliban. Conversely, the 'Awakening' uprising in Iraq balanced Al Qaeda influence in the region."*
BODY-18	*"The design team utilizes the model type that best fits their understanding of the operating environment. Despite the usefulness of these models, they also present several inherent challenges. First, if taken in isolation, models can be misinterpreted as an over-simplification of a complex problem. Second, as detail is added to the model, they can become confusing. Thus, a textual narrative must accompany the diagram to elucidate idiosyncrasies and details of the relationships. Presented in tandem, the narrative and graphic modeling of the operating environment enhances the commander's ability to generate a comprehensive interpretation of a complex dilemma."*
BODY-19	*"[W]henever we propose a solution to a problem, we ought to try as hard as we can to overthrow our solution rather than defend it ... Yet criticism will be fruitful only if we state our problem as clearly as we can and put our solution in a sufficiently definite form - a form in which it can be critically discussed." - K Popper, "The Logic of Scientific Discovery"*
BODY-20	*"In a system, the chains of consequences extend over time and many areas: The effects of action are always multiple ... the point reminds us that disturbing a system will produce several changes." - R. Jervis, "Systems Effects: Complexity in Political and Social Life"*
BODY-21	*"The operational approach is the commander's visualization of those broad actions that will transform a system with observed conditions into a system with desired conditions."*
BODY-22	*"No one starts a war- or rather, no one in his senses ought to do so- without first being clear in his mind what he intends to achieve by that war and how he intends to conduct it." - Clausewitz, "On War"*
BODY-23	*"The changing nature of warfare requires that commanders adapt their plans and methodologies to the operational environment. Reframing is the method within the design process that provides flexibility and versatility in an operational approach."*
BODY-24	*"The number of parts making up the interactively complex system is not the critical issue, and we can't understand these systems by studying their parts in isolation. The*

very essence of the system lies in the interaction between parts and the overall behavior that emerges from the totality of these interactions."

BODY-25 "In this situation, other factors must be analyzed that are relevant to transitioning to the desired system. For example, greater voter turnout may be a more suitable metric for measuring the transformation of the system to better conditions."

BODY-26 "President Uribe's Democratic Security and Defense Policy was an operational approach designed to provide Colombia with a course of action to solve the interactively complex problem."

BODY-27 "A good solution applied with vigor now is better than a perfect solution ten minutes later ..." - Gen. George S. Patton, Jr.

BODY-28 "The capability of NSW leaders to seamlessly integrate and plan with partners to derive approaches to complex situations is the greatest implication for incorporating operational design into the NSW planning process."

BODY-29 "Our struggle to develop a lasting operational approach in Afghanistan that fuses all elements of national power is a harbinger of things to come as we pursue our enemies to other safe havens around the world. The exact solution to this problem will vary with the region that harbors the terrorist network but it will certainly require a broader and more comprehensive view of war-fighting."

BODY-30 "Habitual working relationships with embassy staff, built years in advance, will be the deciding factors in Special Operation's freedom of maneuver on future battle fields."

REPORT DOCUMENTATION PAGE

Form Approved
OMB No. 0704-0188

Public reporting burden for this collection of information is estimated to average 1 hour per response, including the time for reviewing instructions, searching data sources, gathering and maintaining the data needed, and completing and reviewing the collection of information. Send comments regarding this burden estimate or any other aspect of this collection of information, including suggestions for reducing this burden to Washington Headquarters Service, Directorate for Information Operations and Reports, 1215 Jefferson Davis Highway, Suite 1204, Arlington, VA 22202-4302, and to the Office of Management and Budget, Paperwork Reduction Project (0704-0188) Washington, DC 20503.
PLEASE DO NOT RETURN YOUR FORM TO THE ABOVE ADDRESS.

1. REPORT DATE (DD-MM-YYYY)
06-05-2011

2. REPORT TYPE
Master of Military Studies Research Paper

3. DATES COVERED (From - To)
Sep 2010 - May 2011

4. TITLE AND SUBTITLE
Comfortable with Chaos: Incorporating Operational Design into the Naval Special Warfare Planning Process

5a. CONTRACT NUMBER
N/A

5b. GRANT NUMBER
N/A

5c. PROGRAM ELEMENT NUMBER
N/A

6. AUTHOR(S)
LCDR Richard A. Zaszewsi

5d. PROJECT NUMBER
N/A

5e. TASK NUMBER
N/A

5f. WORK UNIT NUMBER
N/A

7. PERFORMING ORGANIZATION NAME(S) AND ADDRESS(ES)
USMC Command and Staff College
Marine Corps University
2076 South Street
Quantico, VA 22134-5068

8. PERFORMING ORGANIZATION REPORT NUMBER
N/A

9. SPONSORING/MONITORING AGENCY NAME(S) AND ADDRESS(ES)
N/A

10. SPONSOR/MONITOR'S ACRONYM(S)
N/A

11. SPONSORING/MONITORING AGENCY REPORT NUMBER
N/A

12. DISTRIBUTION AVAILABILITY STATEMENT
Unlimited

13. SUPPLEMENTARY NOTES
N/A

14. ABSTRACT
The Naval Special Warfare (NSW) mission planning process is an incomplete decision making paradigm that lacks the necessary conceptual components to provide solutions to interactively complex problems in an evolving "multi-nodal" world. The strategic environment is becoming more complex: the world power distribution is shifting as new coalitions form based on diplomatic, military, and economical self interest. Additionally, adversarial state and non-state actors will resort to irregular forms of warfare to challenge the primacy of U.S. Military power. These threats will attempt to gain legitimacy and influence over populations by exploiting the complicated interplay of cyber, energy, economics, technology and the globally connected domains. The interactive complexity of the strategic realm requires NSW leaders to attain a holistic understanding of the environment that their activities impact. Naval Special Warfare must incorporate operational design into its doctrine, processes and organization in order to ensure mission success, maximize effectiveness and maintain its overall relevancy in the strategic domain.

15. SUBJECT TERMS

16. SECURITY CLASSIFICATION OF:

a. REPORT	b. ABSTRACT	c. THIS PAGE
Unclass	Unclass	Unclass

17. LIMITATION OF ABSTRACT
UU

18. NUMBER OF PAGES
29

19a. NAME OF RESPONSIBLE PERSON
Marine Corps University / Command and Staff College

19b. TELEPONE NUMBER (Include area code)
(703) 784-3330 (Admin Office)

Standard Form 298 (Rev. 8-98)
Prescribed by ANSI-Std Z39-18

INSTRUCTIONS FOR COMPLETING SF 298

1. REPORT DATE. Full publication date, including day, month, if available. Must cite at lest the year and be Year 2000 compliant, e.g., 30-06-1998; xx-08-1998; xx-xx-1998.

2. REPORT TYPE. State the type of report, such as final, technical, interim, memorandum, master's thesis, progress, quarterly, research, special, group study, etc.

3. DATES COVERED. Indicate the time during which the work was performed and the report was written, e.g., Jun 1997 - Jun 1998; 1-10 Jun 1996; May - Nov 1998; Nov 1998.

4. TITLE. Enter title and subtitle with volume number and part number, if applicable. On classified documents, enter the title classification in parentheses.

5a. CONTRACT NUMBER. Enter all contract numbers as they appear in the report, e.g. F33615-86-C-5169.

5b. GRANT NUMBER. Enter all grant numbers as they appear in the report, e.g. 1F665702D1257.

5c. PROGRAM ELEMENT NUMBER. Enter all program element numbers as they appear in the report, e.g. AFOSR-82-1234.

5d. PROJECT NUMBER. Enter al project numbers as they appear in the report, e.g. 1F665702D1257; ILIR.

5e. TASK NUMBER. Enter all task numbers as they appear in the report, e.g. 05; RF0330201; T4112.

5f. WORK UNIT NUMBER. Enter all work unit numbers as they appear in the report, e.g. 001; AFAPL30480105.

6. AUTHOR(S). Enter name(s) of person(s) responsible for writing the report, performing the research, or credited with the content of the report. The form of entry is the last name, first name, middle initial, and additional qualifiers separated by commas, e.g. Smith, Richard, Jr.

7. PERFORMING ORGANIZATION NAME(S) AND ADDRESS(ES). Self-explanatory.

8. PERFORMING ORGANIZATION REPORT NUMBER. Enter all unique alphanumeric report numbers assigned by the performing organization, e.g. BRL-1234; AFWL-TR-85-4017-Vol-21-PT-2.

9. SPONSORING/MONITORS AGENCY NAME(S) AND ADDRESS(ES). Enter the name and address of the organization(s) financially responsible for and monitoring the work.

10. SPONSOR/MONITOR'S ACRONYM(S). Enter, if available, e.g. BRL, ARDEC, NADC.

11. SPONSOR/MONITOR'S REPORT NUMBER(S). Enter report number as assigned by the sponsoring/ monitoring agency, if available, e.g. BRL-TR-829; -215.

12. DISTRIBUTION/AVAILABILITY STATEMENT. Use agency-mandated availability statements to indicate the public availability or distribution limitations of the report. If additional limitations/restrictions or special markings are indicated, follow agency authorization procedures, e.g. RD/FRD, PROPIN, ITAR, etc. Include copyright information.

13. SUPPLEMENTARY NOTES. Enter information not included elsewhere such as: prepared in cooperation with; translation of; report supersedes; old edition number, etc.

14. ABSTRACT. A brief (approximately 200 words) factual summary of the most significant information.

15. SUBJECT TERMS. Key words or phrases identifying major concepts in the report.

16. SECURITY CLASSIFICATION. Enter security classification in accordance with security classification regulations, e.g. U, C, S, etc. If this form contains classified information, stamp classification level on the top and bottom of this page.

17. LIMITATION OF ABSTRACT. This block must be completed to assign a distribution limitation to the abstract. Enter UU (Unclassified Unlimited) or SAR (Same as Report). An entry in this block is necessary if the abstract is to be limited.

United States Marine Corps
Command and Staff College
Marine Corps University
2076 South Street
Marine Corps Combat Development Command
Quantico, Virginia 22134-5068

MASTER OF MILITARY STUDIES

COMFORTABLE WITH CHAOS: OPERATIONAL DESIGN IN THE NAVAL SPECIAL WARFARE PLANNING PROCESS

SUBMITTED IN PARTIAL FULFILLMENT
OF THE REQUIREMENTS FOR THE DEGREE OF
MASTER OF MILITARY STUDIES

LCDR Richard A. Zaszewski

AY 10-11

Mentor and Oral Defense Committee Member: Adam Cross
Approved: _____
Date: 11 APL 11

Oral Defense Committee Member: Richard L. DiNardo
Approved: _____
Date: 11 April 2011

Executive Summary

Title: Comfortable with Chaos: Operational Design in the NSW Planning Process

Author: Lieutenant Commander Richard A. Zaszewski

Thesis: The Naval Special Warfare (NSW) mission planning process is an incomplete decision making paradigm that lacks the necessary conceptual components to provide solutions to interactively complex problems in an evolving "multi-nodal" world.

Discussion: The strategic environment is becoming more complex: the world power distribution is shifting as new coalitions form based on diplomatic, military, and economical self interest. Additionally, adversarial state and non-state actors will resort to irregular forms of warfare to challenge the primacy of U.S. Military power. These threats will attempt to gain legitimacy and influence over populations by exploiting the complicated interplay of cyber, energy, economics, technology and the globally connected domains. The interactive complexity of the strategic realm requires NSW leaders to attain a holistic understanding of the environment that their activities impact. Commiserate with this imperative, NSW leaders must collaboratively "understand, plan, act, assess and adapt" with U.S., multinational and host nation partners to devise a comprehensive operational approach that provides a whole of nation solution to interactively complex problems. To address the increasing complexity of the strategic environment, the U.S. Army and Marine Corps adopted operational design into their planning methodologies. Operational design is a conceptual planning paradigm based on Systems Theory that provides solutions to interactively complex problems within the broader context of the operating environment. It is important to understand that operational design does not replace detailed mission planning but planning is incomplete without design. The intent of this paper is not to compare and contrast operational design and the NSW Mission Planning Process but to elucidate the complementary nature of conceptual and detailed planning

Conclusion: Naval Special Warfare must incorporate operational design into its doctrine, processes and organization in order to ensure mission success, maximize effectiveness and maintain its overall relevancy in the strategic domain.

DISCLAIMER

THE OPINIONS AND CONCLUSIONS EXPRESSED HEREIN ARE THOSE OF THE INDIVIDUAL STUDENT AUTHOR AND DO NOT NECESSARILY REPRESENT THE VIEWS OF EITHER THE MARINE CORPS COMMAND AND STAFF COLLEGE OR ANY OTHER GOVERNMENT AGENCY. REFERENCES TO THIS STUDY SHOULD INCLUDE THE FOREGOING STATEMENT.

QUOTATIONS FROM, ABSTRACTIONS FROM, OR REPRODUCTION OF ALL OR ANY PART OF THIS DOCUMENT IS PERMITTED PROVIDED PROPER ACKNOWLEDGEMENT IS MADE.

Illustrations

Page

The Military Decision Making Continuum 23
The Joint Operation Planning Process 24
Operational Design Methodology 24
Causal Loop Diagram 25
The 21st Century World as a "Strategic Ecology" 25

Table of Contents

Page

Disclaimer iii
List of Illustrations iv
Preface vi
Introduction 1
Two Types of Systems 2
The NSW Mission Planning Process 4
    Vignette: Operation HERRICK IV 6
Characteristics of Operational Design 7
Operational Design Methodology 8
    Framing the Environment 8
    Framing the Problem 12
    Considering Operational Approaches 14
    Forging the Design Concept 15
    Reframing 16
    Measuring Transformation 17
    Vignette: Colombia 2002-2006 18
Limitations of Operational Design 20
Implications 21
Conclusion 20

Introduction

"To shape the future force, we must grow leaders who can truly out-think and out-innovate adversaries while gaining trust, understanding and cooperation from our partners in an ever-more complex and dynamic environment."[1]
- The National Military Strategy of the U.S. - 2011

The Naval Special Warfare (NSW) mission planning process is an incomplete decision making paradigm that lacks the necessary conceptual components to provide solutions to interactively complex problems in an evolving "multi-nodal" world.[2] The strategic environment is becoming more complex: the world power distribution is shifting as new coalitions form based on diplomatic, military, and economical self interest. Additionally, adversarial state and non-state actors will resort to irregular forms of warfare to challenge the primacy of U.S. Military power.[3] These threats will attempt to gain legitimacy and influence over populations by exploiting the complicated interplay of cyber, energy, economics, technology and the globally connected domains.

The interactive complexity of the strategic realm requires NSW leaders to attain a holistic understanding of the environment that their activities impact. NSW leaders, in order to maximize the effectiveness of their units' actions, must "understand the population and operating environment, including the complex historical, political, socio-cultural, religious, economic and other causes of violent conflict."[4] Commiserate with this imperative, NSW leaders must collaboratively "understand, plan, act, assess and adapt" with U.S., multinational and host nation partners to devise a comprehensive operational approach that provides a whole of nation solution to interactively complex problems.[5]

The current NSW mission planning process is an analytical problem solving methodology that is designed to provide solutions to *structurally complex* special operations problems.[6] The process is ill equipped to generate conceptual approaches to the interactively complex environment that contains multiple inter-dependant variables as delineated above. To address the increasing complexity of the strategic environment, the U.S. Army and Marine Corps adopted Operational design into their planning methodologies. Operational design is a conceptual planning paradigm based on Systems Theory that provides solutions to interactively complex problems within the broader context of the operating environment. It is important to understand that Operational design does not replace detailed mission planning but planning is incomplete without design.[7] The intent of this paper is not to compare and contrast Operational design and the NSW Mission Planning Process but to elucidate the complementary nature of conceptual and detailed planning. (See Figure 1) As General Mattis stated in reference to this planning dichotomy, "the two processes always are complementary, overlapping, synergistic, and continuous."[8] Operational design enables planners to: anticipate friendly and enemy actions, derive holistic solutions to complex problems, identify enemy critical vulnerabilities and negotiate with inter-agency and coalition partners. To this end, Naval Special Warfare must incorporate Operational design into its doctrine, processes and organization in order to ensure mission success, maximize effectiveness and maintain its overall relevancy in the strategic domain.

Two Types of Systems

"As we have seen, the conduct of war branches out in almost all directions and has no definite limits; while any system, any model, has the finite nature of a synthesis."[9]
– Clausewitz, On War

One must have a basic understanding of the nature of a system in order to solve a problem that arises within that system. Operationally defined, a system contains parts or subsystems that interact with each other and ultimately determine its nature.[10] There are two types of systems that possess unique characteristics - structurally complex (linear) and interactively (nonlinear) complex systems. Structurally complex systems produce "rigid, lockstep and generally predictable behavior."[11] A structurally complex system becomes more complex as the number of parts increases and the more orderly the arrangement of those parts become in relation to each other. A simple example of a structural system is the automobile. The automobile operates in a predictable way and, practically speaking, a problem with the engine can be solved by reducing the engine down to its parts (provided that one is mechanically inclined). Analytic decision making tools, like the NSW mission planning process, are designed to solve structurally complex problems by applying a linear and procedural methodology to derive a solution. The mission (problem) is broken down to its parts by phases, components and variables and analyzed to ultimately determine a suitable course of action.

Interactively complex (nonlinear) systems are inherently unpredictable due to the freedom of action of its subcomponents.[12] The degree of complexity and dynamic behavior of an interactively complex system increases as the subsystems' degrees of freedom increase. One cannot simplify the complexity by reducing the system to its parts because it is the level of interaction of the parts that determines the system's nature. A "simple" example of an interactively complex system is a game of chess between two players. The free will of the players is the condition that makes the system interactively complex. The number of different games that can be played between these two players is 10^{120} – that is the approximate number of electrons in the universe.[13] "We benefit little when we separate the parts of an interactively complex system and study them in isolation. In the act of separation the system loses its coherence and the parts lose their meaning."[14] Social problems like poverty, marginalization and energy dependence are examples of interactively complex problems. Simply stated, any problem that involves the will of people is an interactively complex problem.

Our difficulty in dealing with the insurgencies in Iraq and Afghanistan can be directly attributed to this phenomenon. These interactively complex problems are ill-structured; meaning that there are no obvious solutions. Analytical problem solving methods do not accommodate the interactive relationships of variables in an ill-structured problem like an insurgency. "Reductionism and analysis are not as useful with interactively complex systems because they lose sight of the dynamics between the components. The study of interactively complex systems must be systemic rather than reductionist, and qualitative rather than quantitative, and must use different heuristic approaches rather than analytical problem solving." [15] Therefore, analytical problem solving methodologies alone do not provide sustainable long term solutions to interactively complex problems.

The NSW Mission Planning Process

"Now the elements of the art of war are first, measurement of space; second, estimation of quantities; third, calculations; fourth, comparisons; and fifth, chances of victory. Quantities derive from measurement, figures from quantities, comparisons from figures, and victory from comparisons."[16] *- Sun Tzu, "The Art of War"*

The NSW mission planning process (NSW MPP) adheres to the Joint Operational Planning Process (JOPP).[17] For this reason, this paper will treat the NSW MPP and JOPP interchangeably. This methodology is based upon a classical managerial decision making model: an analytical problem solving methodology that procedurally compares and contrasts potential solutions to problems (See Figure 2). A classical managerial decision making model generally involves seven steps: defining the problem, development of evaluation criteria, identification of alternative courses of action, evaluation of alternatives against criteria, selection of the best alternative, and execution.[18] The process is strictly procedural and rational. The Navy Tactical Training Publication 3-05.2 (Navy SEAL Land Warfare) outlines the NSW MPP in Chapter 2.[19] It is important to note that the Navy publication refers the reader to the Army Operations Process manual (FM 5-0) for additional mission planning guidance but it does not specifically address operational design or solving ill-structured problems.[20]

Analytical decision making models, like the NSW MPP and JOPP, have multiple advantages. Because of its simplicity, the analytical decision making process is effective in time constrained environments. The JOPP is based on the 96 hour planning cycle but the process can be abbreviated should a crisis arise. Analytical decision making models are utilized extensively in Iraq and Afghanistan to conduct time sensitive special operations. Additionally, the simplicity and non-abstract nature of an analytical decision making process enables its implementation by inexperienced members of the tactical elements. Lastly, the NSW MPP is useful in the synchronization of multiple maneuver elements in time and space to achieve a desired objective.

Analytical decision making processes attempt to influence events before they occur therefore, they must rely on multiple layers of assumptions regarding the operating environment.[21] First, the analytical decision making process assumes that a problem is definable and the Commander's guidance and intent clearly articulates the end state.[22] Second, the analytical models assume that it is possible to anticipate future events since all information required for a decision is readily available and all options can be evaluated to determine an optimal solution.[23] Third, it assumes the stability of the operating environment and the availability of time. Thus the chosen course of action will be the most direct solution to the problem.[24] Lastly, the analytical decision making process assumes full knowledge and participation of all key stakeholders involved in the decision making process. The NATO led, Helmand River Campaign in Afghanistan from 2005 to 2007 is an example where operational design was not employed and the assumptions delineated above proved false when utilizing traditional analytical problem solving approaches to deal with an interactively complex situation.

The British 16th Air Assault Brigade launched Operation HERRICK IV to southern Helmand in 2006. Prior to this point, U.S. Special Forces conducted direct action raids to kill or capture senior Taliban and Al Qaeda leaders. The British forces deployed to the region under confusing orders and lacking a coherent purpose to their mission. Senior British politicians supported a counter-drug approach to stabilize a region that produced a significant portion of Afghanistan's opium export.[25] Meanwhile, British military personnel were planning on conducting counter-insurgency operations while under intense hostile fire.[26] The lack of a clear direction amongst British leaders stemmed from a lack of consensus on the root cause of the problem in Helmand. What resulted was a disharmonious and ill-synchronized approach to dealing with the insurgency in the region. The lack of clear direction was compounded by the lack of participation of the local political leadership. "There was essentially no 'Kabul-backed' regional government in the province when the British arrived; this created a number of obstacles, as Afghan governmental representatives were often not available to discuss operations or deal with reconstruction."[27] The absence of these key stakeholders in the planning process resulted in a dearth of information regarding potential solutions to Helmand's strife. To make matters worse for the 16th Air Assault Brigade, the operating environment shifted due to friendly and enemy influence. British Commanders initially desired to deploy company or platoon sized elements to secure population centers but in a deliberate way to prevent operational over-reach. British higher level decision makers, however, chose to increase the number of the tactical elements resulting in sustainability problems for the isolated garrisons. The Taliban quickly took advantage of the opportunity to strike at the over stretched British and launched an intense campaign that further restricted the British ability to interact with the populace. Operation HERRICK IV was a tactical – military success for the British but their inability to conceptually grasp the interactive complexity of the insurgency in Helmand failed to provide a sustainable solution to the problem.

Characteristics of Operational design

> *"Commanders at all levels in ongoing and future armed conflicts will continue to face highly complex, dynamic and novel problem situations for which the known and practiced solutions may not suffice."*[28] *– JWFC Doctrine Pamphlet*

> *"Design culture is inherently participative and pluralistic. It encourages continual reflection and discourse to develop inter-subjective (shared) meaning. The design culture is not seeking optimality against a set of measures of effectiveness, but rather improvement."*[29] *– The Art of Design*

Operational design is a deliberative process that enables a commander and his staff to apply critical and creative thinking approaches to interactively complex problems.[30] The conversational methodology that design embodies creates a shared understanding about the problem and shared commitment to the broad operational approach.[31] Operational design while complementary to detailed planning has multiple unique characteristics that set it apart from traditional analytical processes. First, Operational design is utilized to develop understanding about interactively complex problems for which there is no inherent logic. Decision makers typically solve problems intuitively or analytically; an interactively complex problem cannot immediately be solved using either one of these methods.[32] Second, Operational design is a conceptual decision making paradigm that views the operating environment as an *open system* – a system that interacts within the broader confines of a larger system.[33] Operational design thus assumes an expansionist view of the operating environment. Third, Operational design focuses on problem framing vice problem solving. Problem framing involves understanding the root cause of the problem to insure that the correct problem is addressed. Analytical decision making models focus on identifying a solution to a problem. Fourth, the design process, while requiring some level of structure, is focused on building an understanding of the environment vice building "products" for comparison. Finally, the tangible product of the design process is the *design concept*. The design concept is the commander's visualization of a broad approach to addressing the problem.[34] The design concept inputs the detailed planning process for refinement and execution.

Operational Design Methodology

Operational design is a process that involves six formal steps: framing the environment, framing the problem, considering operational approaches, forging the design concept, execution and assessment and reframing. (See Figure 3) The process is iterative and procedural but the complexity of the problem may require the commander to regress to earlier steps or proceed to advanced steps until a broad solution emerges. Simply stated Operational design is non-linear in application and should not involve lock step rigidity in its execution. This characteristic must be adhered for creative and critical thinking to flourish amongst the members of the design team. Holistic self-learning about the nature of the system is more important than prematurely moving to a solution.

Framing the Environment

"The man responsible for evaluating the whole must bring to his task the quality of intuition that perceives the truth at every point. Otherwise a chaos of opinions and considerations would arise and fatally entangle judgment."[35] *– Clausewitz, On War*

The Operational design process begins with receipt of a mission or planning guidance from higher authority. At this point, the commander and his staff gain an "initial impression of the mess" and begin erecting a framework of the complexity. If no solutions are immediately evident and the problem is sufficiently complex, the commander forms a design team that includes key stakeholders in the problem. Design members should be selected for their capability to contribute as well as their involvement in the mission. If feasible, the tactical leadership responsible for detailed planning and execution should be incorporated. Examples of key stakeholders included on the design team are inter-agency personnel and field experts such as scientists or technicians. The commander must be mindful of the size of the design team as the most effective decision making groups have between five and six members. Design teams comprised of nine personnel are still effective but groups of 20 or more are completely ineffectual.[36] Members of the design team have assigned responsibilities. Minimum key roles are team leader, request for information (RFI) manager, time keeper, notes keeper and graphic annotator. Liaison teams are dispatched to connect with distant stakeholders not located with the commander. Episodic video teleconferences between the liaison and design teams are useful in conveying critical information from out stations. Of particular concern when forming the design team are operational security concerns and institutional boundaries that may preclude certain key stakeholders from membership. The commander should make every attempt through formal channels to include ostracized key stakeholders that are critical to framing the environment.

When framing the environment, the first question the design team attempts to answer is: what are the *current conditions* of the *observed system* and what is wrong with it? "An observed system is a term of reference for the current state of the system as we see it and understand it."[37] The answer to the first question gives a contextual understanding of the system and why it should be influenced. The design team seeks the nature of the observed system and its conditions by analyzing its actors, tendencies, potentials and basic relationships.

- Actors are those individuals or communities that comprise the system and attempt to advance their individual or collective interest.[38] There are *relevant* and *key actors*. *Relevant actors* are manifold; they can be government, non-government, criminal, military, insurgent or business etc. *Key actors* are fundamental to the behavior of the system and influence it more profoundly than relevant actors.[39] The design team must identify what key actors will support and those that will resist change to the desired system.

- "*Tendencies* are predictions about how the system will behave if left alone."[40] For example, the Japanese would have continued their Imperial expansion in the Pacific if the United States did not respond to their aggression in World War Two.

- "*Potentials* are the limits to which a system can be influenced by our actions and those of others."[41] For example, Afghanistan does not have the potential to become an industrial power by 2014 when the U.S. departs the region.

- "*Relationships* are the linkages that connect the interaction of the actors that make up the system."[42] The relationships can be reinforcing (positive) or balancing (negative). For example, civilian casualties due to coalition air strikes in Afghanistan reinforce the legitimacy of Taliban. Conversely, the "Awakening" uprising in Iraq balanced Al Qaeda influence in the region.

A causal loop diagram is one type of schematic that depicts the relationships of the actors within a system. It is a useful tool that enhances the design team's visualization of the operational environment. (See Figure 4) "Building explicit conceptual models of the situation help promote understanding among stakeholders of the various forces at work."[43] Causal loop diagrams are one of many graphical depictions used to interpret the environment; others include network, mind mapping and business models among others. (See Figure 5) The design team utilizes the model type that best fits their understanding of the operating environment. Despite the usefulness of these models, they also present several inherent challenges. First, if taken in isolation, models can be misinterpreted as an over-simplification of a complex problem. Second, as detail is added to the model, they can become confusing. Thus, a textual narrative must accompany the diagram to elucidate idiosyncrasies and details of the relationships. Presented in tandem, the narrative and graphic modeling of the operating environment enhances the commander's ability to generate a comprehensive interpretation of a complex dilemma. The initial "environmental frame" is derived from the graphic and textual representation of the observed system.

When framing the environment, the second question the design team asks is: what are the *feasible* and *better conditions* of the *desired system*? "The *desired system* consists of those conditions that, if achieved, meet the objectives of policy, orders, guidance, and directives issued to the commander."[44] The answer to the second question builds a better appreciation for the purpose and the approximate scope of the action to be taken. The usage of *feasible* and *better* to describe the conditions of the desired system is significant because it underscores that available time and resources are critical to the determination of a suitable approach. These terms imply that the chosen operational approach "satisfices" the problem and may not be the optimal solution.[45] The environmental frame is developed and refined to depict how the system could "trend" from the observable (current) conditions to the desired (future) conditions. The environmental frame results in the generation of a tangible end state of the desired system and an articulation of its desired conditions.

Framing the Problem

"[W]henever we propose a solution to a problem, we ought to try as hard as we can to overthrow our solution rather than defend it...Yet criticism will be fruitful only if we state our problem as clearly as we can and put our solution in a sufficiently definite form – a form in which it can be critically discussed." [46] – K. Popper, *"The Logic of Scientific Discovery"*

In problem framing, the commander and his design team transition from developing a deep understanding of the operating environment to determining the correct problem and its underlying causes. "Problem framing involves understanding and isolating the root causes of conflict – defining the essence of a complex, ill-structured problem."[47] The design team transforms the graphic and textual environmental frame into the problem frame by conducting an in depth analysis of the system's actors and its tendencies and potential. The problem frame exceeds a superficial understanding of the relationships within the system. The design team, during problem framing, analyses multiple factors: the leadership, tension and competition, roles, agendas and alliances and patterns of behavior (L-TRAP) amongst the actors in the system.

- Leadership: Who are the friendly, enemy and neutral leaders in the system – both formal and informal? What leaders support and deter movement of the observed system to the desired system? Who are the most capable leaders? What are their patterns of life?

- Tensions and Competition: "Tension is the resistance or friction among and between actors." [48] Competition, for the purpose of this paper, is a form of tension between otherwise amiable individuals or groups. Nevertheless, competition is a source of friction that may impede the system's movement to more desirable conditions. "By analyzing these tensions, the commander identifies the problem that the design will ultimately solve."[49] Tension and competition is identified through pattern analysis of the actors.

- Roles: What functional roles do key actors play within the system? What utility do the key actors bring to the health and sickness of the system? What are the indirect results if a key actor is removed? Who will assume these roles?

- Agendas and Alliances: What are the key actors' underlying motivations? What are the overt and covert alliances amongst actors? How can the force leverage their agendas to gain genuine buy in and collaboratively move to the desired system?

- Patterns of Behavior: What are the individual patterns of behavior of key actors? Where and when are they most vulnerable – most capable?

The L-TRAP analysis method enables the design team to anticipate friendly and enemy actions, develop holistic approaches to the problem, identify enemy critical vulnerabilities and increase negotiating leverage with inter-agency and coalition partners. It is important that the commander and his design team continue to challenge their hypotheses regarding the relationships of key actors and the potential and tendencies of the system. The problem frame results in a statement that temporally and spatially describes the requirements for transformation. Additionally, the problem statement identifies when and where to anticipate changes and transitions in the operational environment.[50]

Considering Operational Approaches

"In a system, the chains of consequences extend over time and many areas: The effects of action are always multiple...the point reminds us that disturbing a system will produce several changes."[51] *- R. Jervis, "Systems Effects: Complexity in Political and Social Life"*

"In this multi-nodal world, the military's contribution to American leadership must be about more than power – it must be about our approach to exercising power."[52]
- The National Military Strategy of the U.S. - 2011

The operational approach is the commander's visualization of those broad actions that will transform a system with observed conditions into a system with desired conditions.[53] The commander and the design team consider combinations of military, inter-agency, host nation and diplomatic approaches that may result in the desired conditions. Furthermore, the design team assesses the direct and indirect impact the operational approach will have on the system. As the operational approach is being refined, relevant subject matter expertise is enlisted to support the design team. In developing the operational approach, the design team links tasks and purposes with the desired system and articulates the operational approach by using lines of operation, lines of effort or other elements of design.[54] Most importantly, the design team assesses how the effectiveness of the operational approach should be measured. What factors and conditions indicate that the system in trending toward desired conditions? Measuring effectiveness and performance of the operational approach is discussed later in this text.

The commander and his staff consider funding, asset availability and authorities to develop an operational approach that is feasible. An operational approach may require a force to have niche capabilities that necessitate specialized training or equipment. The commander must determine if additional funding is required to provide this capability. Additionally, the commander must be aware if an operational approach requires the deployment or extraction of the force with additional or unique assets. Lastly, the commander must have the authority to employ an operational approach and coordinate with adjacent elements supporting the operation. If there are discrepancies in funding, assets or authorities, the commander has the option to adjust the operational approach or request additional support from higher.

Analyzing the system with the L-TRAP paradigm enables the design team to anticipate friendly, enemy and neutral reaction to the operational approach; thus depicting the methodology for maintaining initiative. The design team analyzes risk throughout the design process and attempts to mitigate risk during the design phase by leveraging inter-agency and host nation partners. "Collaboration, coordination, and cooperation among multinational military and civilian partners are essential to identifying potential options for mitigating risk, conserving resources, and achieving unity of effort."[55] If necessary, the approach is re-adjusted to exploit enemy vulnerabilities while avoiding enemy strengths.

Forging the Design Concept

"No one starts a war – or rather, no one in his senses ought to do so – without first being clear in his mind what he intends to achieve by that war and how he intends to conduct it."[56]
- Clausewitz, "On War"

The design concept is the link between the abstract nature of Operational design and the reality of the detailed planning process. In essence, the design concept is the commander's articulated vision for moving the observed system to the desired system. The commander's actual guidance is mission dependant and can vary significantly. Commonly, the design concept includes the following: the problem statement, a mission narrative, initial commander's intent, planning guidance to include assumptions and operational limitations and any products from the design process (textual and graphic). "The design concept describes the desired conditions and the combinations of potential broad actions in time, space, and purpose to achieve the desired system."[57] The design concept is injected into the detailed planning process and the course of action is extrapolated. Concurrently during the detailed planning process, the design team continues to refine the design concept within the context of the operating environment. The design concept is analyzed and assessed throughout the planning and execution phases. If at any time the operating environment invalidates the design concept, the commander and his staff must reframe their hypothesis of the operational approach.

Reframing

"And as water shapes it flow in accordance with the ground, so an army manages its victory in accordance with the situation of the enemy. And as water has no constant form, there are in war no constant conditions."[58] *-Sun Tzu, "The Art of War"*

The changing nature of warfare requires that commanders adapt their plans and methodologies to the operational environment. Reframing is the method within the design process that provides flexibility and versatility in an operational approach. The commander and his staff make the decision to reframe the problem and resolution when the original understanding of the environment or problem changes. "At any time during the operations process, the decision to reframe can stem from significant changes to understanding, the conditions of the operational environment, or the end state."[59] Reframing is akin to what the renowned psychologist and philosopher Thomas Kuhn deemed a "paradigm shift." A paradigm is the framework that scientists use to solve a set of difficult problems.[60] A "shift" is required when the current paradigm or understanding is no longer relevant. The commander and his staff must continually assess and evaluate their understanding of the existing problem and the operational approach they are employing to address that problem.[61]

In the "Art of Design," the U.S. Army states that reframing is triggered in three ways: "a major event causes a —catastrophic change in the operational environment, a scheduled periodic review shows a problem, or an assessment and reflection challenges understanding of the existing problem and the relevance of the operational approach."[62] Reframing changes the understanding of the problem, requires the commander to revisit problem framing and involves the refinement of one or more key aspects of the design concept. For instance, reframing resulted in a several shifts from enemy centric approaches to population centric approaches since the commencement of Operation ENDURING FREEDOM. The adjustment in the Afghanistan operational approach permeated all aspects of the design concept and resulted in tactical directives to subordinate units that reflected the commander's new vision to achieve the desired end state.

Measuring Transformation

"The number of parts making up the interactively complex system is not the critical issue, and we can't understand these systems by studying their parts in isolation. The very essence of the system lies in the interaction between parts and the overall behavior that emerges from the totality of these interactions."[63]- JWFC Doctrine Pamphlet, "Design in Military Operations"

Measuring the transformation of the observed system to the desired system is critical to anticipating changes in the operational environment, identifying reframing triggers and signifying when desired conditions are met. "Commanders continuously assess the operational environment and the progress of operations, and compare them to their initial vision and commander's intent."[64] Leveraging all sources of intelligence, commanders challenge their hypotheses and adjust their operational approach to ensure the desired end state is achieved. The measurement of effectiveness and performance of a particular operational approach is frequently mishandled.[65] A common mistake is to measure for desired conditions while not analyzing those factors that indicate a trend toward the desired system. Until recently, Joint Inter-agency Task Force – South (JIATF-S) measured the performance of their counter-drug strategy by the quantity of cocaine and money seized during its operations.[66] These metrics misled planners into believing the efficacy of their strategy, overemphasized a simplified approach to a complex problem and did not alert the task force to the increase in complexity of the operating environment. SAMS design planners working with JIATF-S developed new measures of effectiveness and performance that provided relevant data based on the movement of the entire system to a desired state. The operating environment must be analyzed holistically, examining as many system attributes as possible to determine how relevant actors interact and conditions change. From this perspective, quantifying the number of enemy significant activity (SIGACT) events does not accurately measure the performance of a counter-insurgency strategy when the underlying problem is host nation government legitimacy in the eyes of the populace. In this situation, other factors must be analyzed that are relevant to transitioning to the desired system. For example, greater voter turnout may be a more suitable metric for measuring the transformation of the system to better conditions.

Colombia – Operational design at Work

In 2002, when President Alvaro Uribe Velez took office, Colombia was enduring a multi-faceted and interactively complex strategic situation. Three major insurgent groups battled with Colombian forces for legitimacy. First, the *Fuerzas Armadas Revolucionarias de Colombia* or FARC (Revolutionary Armed Forces of Colombia) controlled a vast region in Colombia – the *Zona de Despeje*.[67] From this safe haven, the FARC organized attacks on government forces and coordinated illicit narcotics operations. The safe haven also afforded the FARC with a training and organizational base. Additionally, the FARC received funding, training and equipping support from international state and non-state entities endeared to their cause.[68] Second, the Ejercito de Liberacion Nacional or ELN (National Liberation Army) conducted subversive attacks on Colombian institutions and organizations to further their Marxist cause. While not as prolific or grand as the FARC, the ELN represented an additional security problem to the Colombian government that required alternative approaches. Lastly, the Autodefensas Unidas de Colombia or AUC (Self-defense Forces of Colombia) was a home grown paramilitary movement that formed due to the inefficacy of Colombian government security operations to combat the FARC and ELN. The AUC carried out vigilante and terror attacks on FARC – ELN operators and supporters. Despite fighting for the survival of Colombia's democratic institution, the AUC increasingly resorted to the drug trade to fund their operations and ultimately challenged the legitimacy of government forces and institutions. Against this back drop, President Uribe took office and designed a comprehensive strategy to tackle the "wicked" problem.

President Uribe designed an operational approach that significantly contrasted with the strategy of his predecessor, President Andreas Pastrana. President Pastrana focused on negotiating a settlement with the FARC and ELN, perceiving that the underlying cause of Colombia's strife was the narcotics trade.[69] Attempting to placate the FARC, President Pastrana imparted the *Zona de Despeje* to the insurgent group - a region as big as the country of Switzerland. Pastrana's strategy, *Plan Colombia,* was nothing more than a list of social ills with proposed solutions; however, President Uribe's *Democratic Security and Defense Policy* was an operational approach designed to provide Colombia with a course of action to solve the interactively complex problem.[70]

First, Uribe's policy framed the environment – it recognized the interactive complexity of "'terrorism; the illegal drugs trade; illicit finance; traffic of arms, ammunition, and explosives; kidnapping and extortion; and homicide.'"[71] Second, Uribe's administration framed the problem as a lack of personal security for all Colombians that stemmed from "the state's absence from large swaths of the national territory."[72] Third, the Colombian government designed an operational approach to ensure national integration and sovereignty.[73] Ultimately, Uribe's design concept was to consolidate control of national territory. Security forces would physically reestablish control of contested areas then other government institutions would embark on social and fiscal initiatives to consolidate these gains.[74] The shared understanding of the problem frame resulted in unity of effort amongst the various departments of the Colombian government – unattainable by previous presidents. From 2002 to 2006, the Uribe administration reframed their understanding of the problem and challenged their hypotheses as the operating environment changed. In conclusion, President Uribe designed an elastic strategy that improved the Colombian system that still endures today.

Limitations of Operational design

"A good solution applied with vigor now is better than a perfect solution ten minutes later..."[75]

- *Gen. George S. Patton, Jr.*

Time consumption is the greatest limitation of the operational design process; therefore, it has limited application when conducting special operations in time sensitive environments. Certain crisis situations, such as rescuing a prisoner of war (POW), require that NSW forces alert, deploy and execute in a very short period of time due to the nature of perishable intelligence, enemy action and external political factors. In these instances, a profound understanding of the operating environment is a lesser priority to the successful outcome of the mission. Eliminating operational design from the decision making process during time sensitive missions results in a quicker turnaround for execution but the absence of design results in a superficial understanding of the underlying causes of the problem. "Planning without design may not result in as deep an understanding as that resulting from the design process."[76] Conducting operational design in parallel with detailed planning and execution is an alternative option to completely removing design from the decision making process. "A unit may already be planning and executing when the commander recognizes a need for design."[77] This is the most difficult situation for implementing operational design due to the number of moving parts and the amount of "catch up" required of the design team. In this situation, the commander must choose the members of his design team based on the members' knowledge of the current situation and their "track record" of designing together.[78] The commander, to prepare for such scenarios, should have a standing design team prepared to integrate into crisis action planning. If there is no standing design team, the commander must balance regional expertise and knowledge of the design process when choosing team members.

Implications

The capability of NSW leaders to seamlessly integrate and plan with partners to derive approaches to complex situations is the greatest implication for incorporating operational design into the NSW planning process. Several steps must be taken to accomplish this objective. First, system theory and operational design must be infused into NSW education and training. System theory underpins design with concepts and terminology. This paper superficially addresses some key aspects of system theory but NSW leaders must attain a deeper understanding of systems in order to become capable practitioners of design. Additionally, operational design must be introduced to NSW leaders at all echelons. Training should focus on teaching design through planning exercises. Utilizing simulations and hypothetical scenarios, NSW leaders will learn how to model systems and devise operational approaches to complex problems. U.S. Army SAMS students learn operational design during three – two week long practical exercises that encourage experimentation and reflection on the practice of design. NSW should utilize a similar methodology, starting in SEAL Qualification Training (SQT) that progressively teaches its leaders how to practice design.

Second, NSW should deploy O-5 commanders who are adept at operational design to countries where NSW tactical elements are conducting theatre support activities. These commanders, stationed at the U.S. embassy, should embed with country team planners to assist them with devising operational approaches to regional problems. Deploying NSW operational designers to country teams will have immediate impacts on operations and strategy. The commanders will assist the country team planners in formulating whole of nation approaches that incorporate NSW participation. Additionally, these planners will gain a deeper appreciation of the complexity of the situation thus enabling them to better direct the tactical and operational employment of NSW elements.

Conclusion

Naval Special Warfare's inherent flexibility and its cultural aversion to doctrine create ripe conditions for the inclusion of operational design into the NSW mission planning process. As the employment pendulum swings from sustained combat operations to theatre engagement, NSW leaders must be capable of integrating and planning with a myriad of partners to devise lasting solutions to complex problems. The future security of our homeland will not be measured by how many enemy are killed, nor by how many mouths are fed, but in essence how the United States is able to blend these two seemingly disparate lines of effort into one consolidated strategy. Our struggle to develop a lasting operational approach in Afghanistan that fuses all elements of national power is a harbinger of things to come as we pursue our enemies to other safe havens around the world. The exact solution to this problem will vary with the region that harbors the terrorist network but it will certainly require a broader and more comprehensive view of war-fighting. Our future strategy for counter-terrorist operations must account for the interactive complexity of a host nation's infrastructure and economy as well as the enemy's capabilities. Operational design, if incorporated into the NSW mission planning process, will enable NSW leaders to develop a more complete understanding of the local, regional and national geo-political terrain to de-code this complex enigma. Additionally, the future pursuit of our nation's enemies abroad will require a more collaborative approach with our inter-agency and coalition partners. We must fully grasp their institutional concerns and incorporate these variables into the overall analysis. Habitual working relationships with embassy staff, built years in advance, will be the deciding factors in Special Operation's freedom of maneuver on future battle fields. Special Operations Forces can no longer view its part in this fight as a single compound assault executed in a vacuum.

Figure 1: The Military Decision Making Continuum – Operational design is the "left side" of detailed mission planning

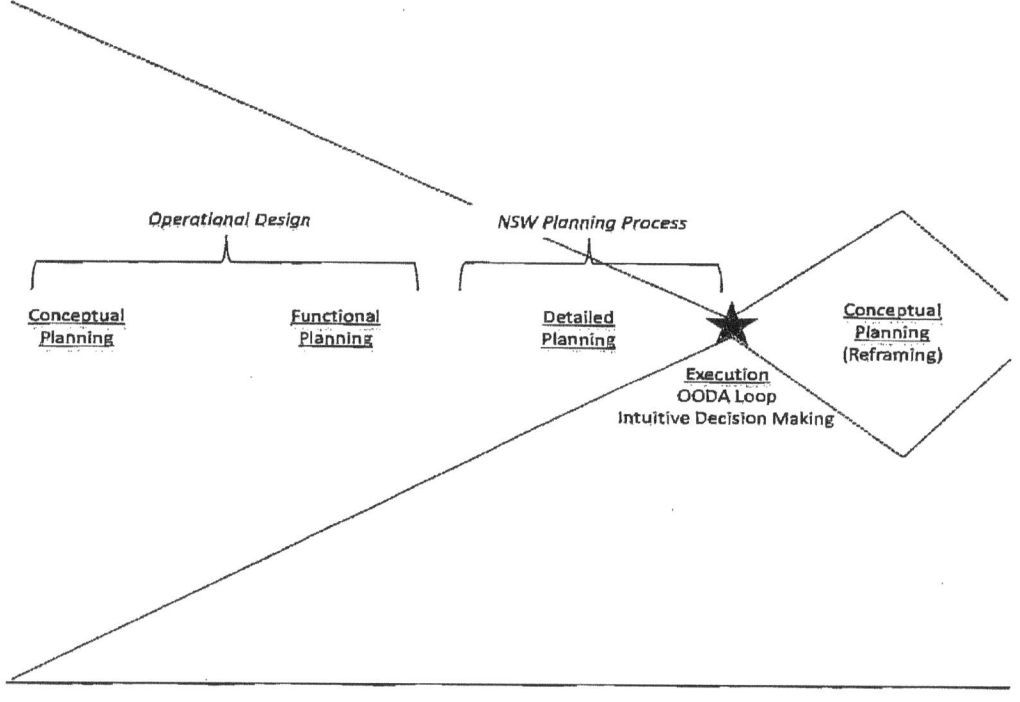

Figure 2: The Joint Operation Planning Process. Taken from NSW Tactics and Training Publication 3-5.2 "SEAL Land Warfare"

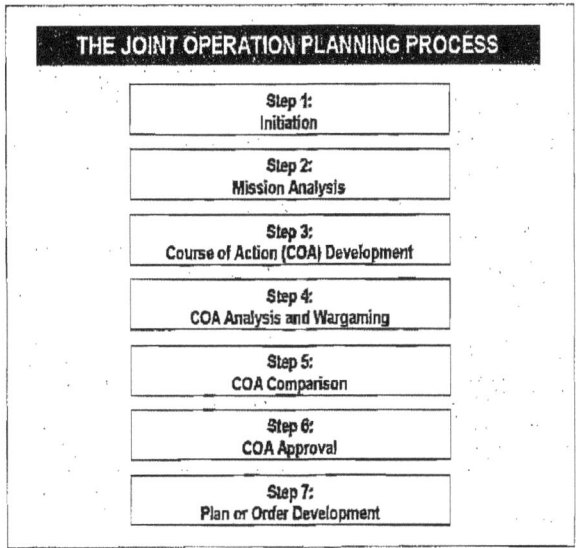

Figure 2-1. The Joint Operation Planning Process (from Joint Pub 5-0, Fig III-3, p. III-20)

Figure 3: Operational Design Methodology (utilizing U.S. Army and U.S.M.C. design components)

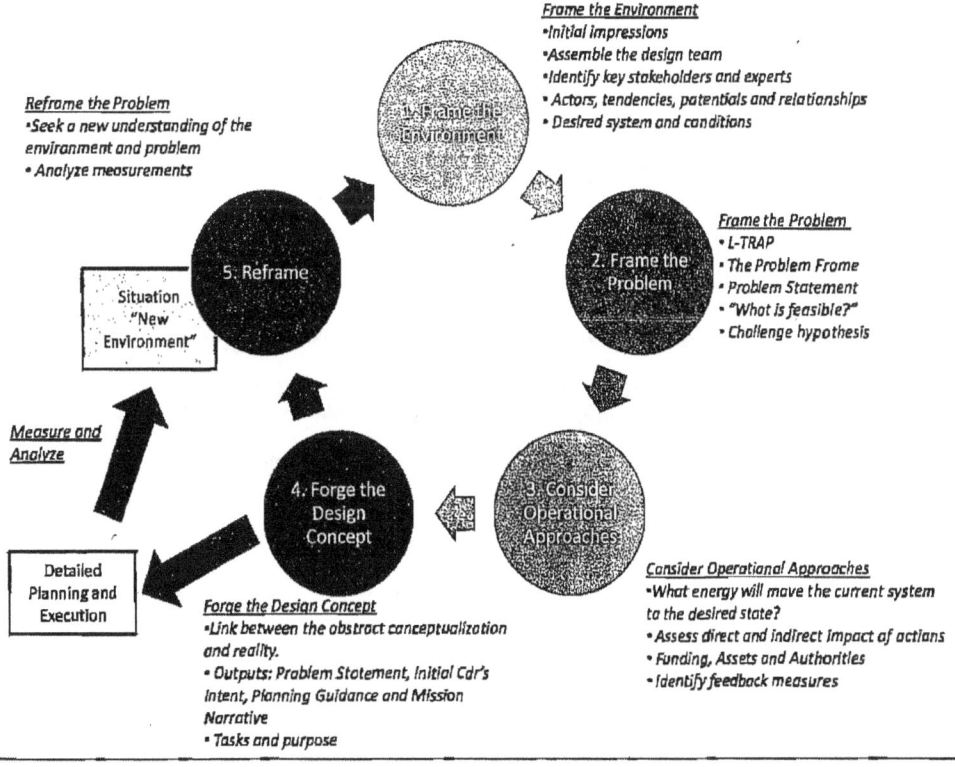

Figure 4: A sample causal loop diagram depicting the inter-active complexity of a hypothetical insurgency. (Taken from training workshop at U.S.M.C University and attributed to P.V. Riper)

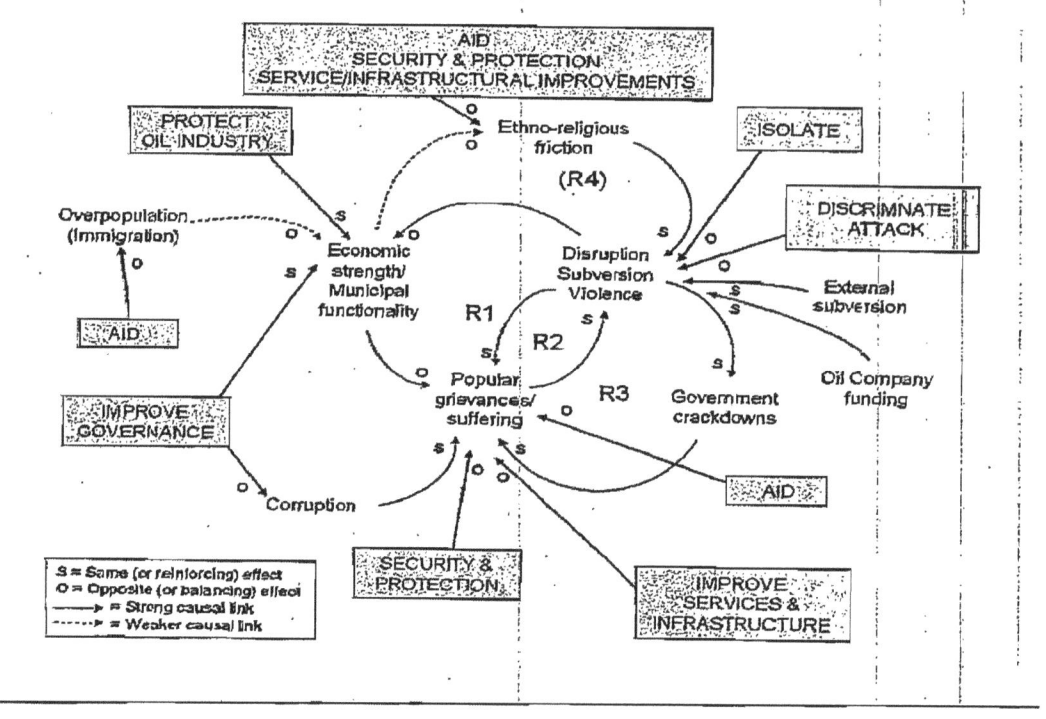

Figure 5: The 21st Century World as a "Strategic Ecology" (U.S. National Strategy Concept, 18 October 2010)

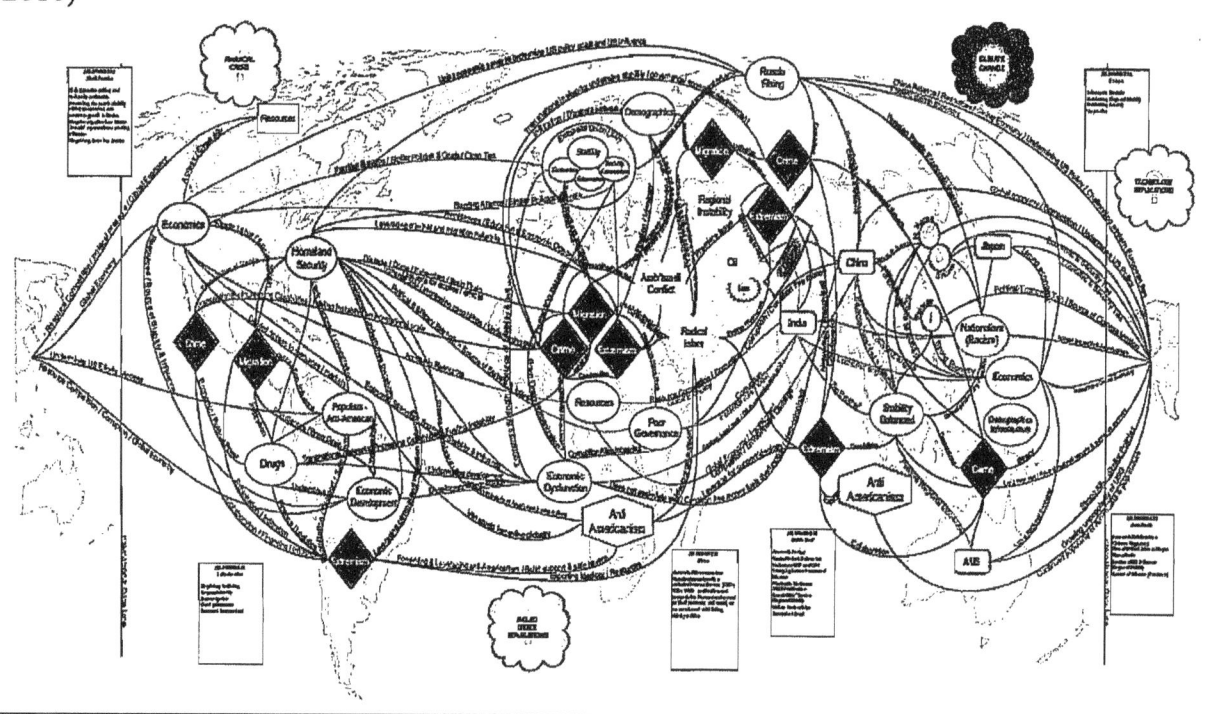

Endnotes:

[1] U.S. Department of Defense, *The National Military Strategy of the United States of America*, 2011, p. 16
[2] Paul K. Van Riper, *An Introduction to System Theory and Decision Making*, 2010, p. 1, Interactively complex (nonlinear) systems are inherently unpredictable due to the freedom of action of its subcomponents.
[3] U.S. Joint Forces Command, *Irregular Warfare: Countering Irregular Threats*, Version 2.0, 17 May 2010, p. 4
[4] Ibid, p. 5
[5] Ibid, p. 11
[6] Van Riper, p.1 Structurally complex systems produce "rigid, lockstep and generally predictable behavior." A structurally complex system becomes more complex as the number of parts increases and the more orderly the arrangement of those parts become in relation to each other.
[7] U.S. Joint Forces Command, *Design in Military Operations*, 2010, p. 29
[8] U.S. Army, School of Advanced Military Studies, *Art of Design*, Version 2, 2010, p. 1
[9] Carl Von Clausewitz, *On War*, (New Jersey: Princeton University Press, 1984), p. 86
[10] Van Riper, p. 1
[11] Ibid, p. 1
[12] Ibid, p. 1
[13] Ibid, p. 5
[14] Ibid, p. 1
[15] *Art of Design*, p. 13
[16] Sun Tzu, *The Art of War*, (New York: Oxford University Press, 1963) p. 88
[17] U.S. Navy Tactical Training Publication 3-05.2, *SEAL Land Warfare*, Dec 2008, p. 2-4
[18] M.H. Bazerman, *Judgment in Managerial Decision Making*, p. 4
[19] U.S. Navy Tactical Training Publication 3-05.2, Chapter 2
[20] Ibid, p. 2-9
[21] *The Art of Design*, pp. 11
[22] Ibid, Location pp. 12
[23] Ibid, Location pp. 12
[24] Ibid, Location pp. 12
[25] Marston, D and Carter Malkasian, *Counterinsurgency in Modern Warfare*, (New York: Osprey Publishing, 2008), p. 237
[26] Ibid, p. 237
[27] Ibid, p. 237
[28] *Design in Military Operations*, p. 8
[29] *The Art of Design*, p. 14
[30] Operational design (DOD) is a methodology for applying critical and creative thinking to understand, visualize, and describe complex, ill-structured problems and develop approaches to solve them.
[31] John F. Schmitt, *A Systemic Concept for Operational Design*, Marine Corps Combat Development Command, Concepts and Plans Division, Marine Corps Warfighting Lab Concept Paper, Aug. 2006, p. 19
[32] Interactively complex problems are sometimes referred to as "wicked" or "ill-structured." For a more comprehensive definition of "wicked problems" see *A Systemic Concept for Operational Design*.
[33] *Art of Design*, p. 326
[34] U.S. Army Training and Doctrine Command, Field Manual 5-0, *Operations Process*, (Fort Monroe, Virginia, March 2010), Chapter 3, p. 3-12
[35] Clausewitz, p. 112
[36] *Art of Design*, p. 25
[37] *Design in Military Operations*, p. 8
[38] Ibid, p. 9
[39] Ibid, p. 8
[40] Ibid, p. 8
[41] Ibid, p. 8
[42] Ibid, p. 8
[43] J.F. Schmitt, p. 24
[44] Ibid, p. 9

[45] "Satisfices" is a Systems Theory term that co-joins the words satisfy and sufficient
[46] K. Popper, *The Logic of Scientific Discovery*, (London, Routledge, 2002), p. xix
[47] *Operations Process*, p. 3-10
[48] Ibid, p. 3-10
[49] *Design in Military Operations*, p. 12
[50] Ibid, p. 3-11
[51] Robert Jervis, *System Effects: Complexity in Political and Social Life*, (New Jersey: Princeton University Press, 1997), p. 10
[52] The National Military Strategy of the United States of America, 2011, p. 5
[53] *Design in Military Operations*, p. 15
[54] Ibid, p. 14
[55] Ibid, p.15
[56] Clausewitz, p. 579
[57] *Design in Military Operations*, p. 16
[58] Sun Tzu, p. 101
[59] *Art of Design*, p. 141
[60] Alexander Bird, "Thomas Kuhn," *The Stanford Encyclopedia of Philosophy*, (Fall 2008 Edition), p. 2
[61] *Art of Design*, p. 131
[62] Ibid, p. 142
[63] *Design in Military Operations*, p.26
[64] Department of the Army, U.S. Army Field Manual 3-24-2, *Counterinsurgency Doctrine*, (Apr 2009), p. 96
[65] Measure of Performance (DOD): An MOP is criterion used to assess friendly actions that is tied to measuring task accomplishment (JP 1-02). MOPs confirm or deny that the task has been correctly performed. An example of a MOP is "How many people registered to vote at the school this week?"
Measure of Effectiveness (DOD): An MOE is criterion used to assess changes in system behavior, capability, or operational environment that is tied to measuring the attainment of an end state, achievement of an objective, or creation of an effect (JP 3-0). An example of a MOE is "Did the well project provide clean drinking water to the village?"
[66] *Art of Design*, p. 157
[67] Ibid, p. 40
[68] Ibid, p. 50
[69] Ibid, p. 51
[70] Ibid, p. 54
[71] Ibid, p. 54
[72] Ibid, p. 54
[73] Ibid, p. 54
[74] Ibid, p. 54
[75] Owen Connelly, *On War and Leadership; The Words of Combat Commanders from Frederick the Great to Norman Schwarzkopf*, (New Jersey: Princeton University Press, 2005) p. 125
[76] *Design in Military Operations*, p. 15
[77] *Art of design*, p. 22
[78] Ibid, p. 22

www.ingramcontent.com/pod-product-compliance
Lightning Source LLC
Chambersburg PA
CBHW080603090426
42735CB00016B/3323